Wicca Book of Spells

----- ✥✥✥✥ -----

A Spell book for Beginners to Advanced Wiccans, Witches and other Practitioners of Magic

© Copyright 2017 - All rights reserved.

The contents of this book may not be reproduced, duplicated or transmitted without direct written permission from the author.

Under no circumstances will any legal responsibility or blame be held against the publisher for any reparation, damages, or monetary loss due to the information herein, either directly or indirectly.

Legal Notice:

This book is copyright protected. This is only for personal use. You cannot amend, distribute, sell, use, quote or paraphrase any part or the content within this book without the consent of the author.

Disclaimer Notice:

Please note the information contained within this document is for educational and entertainment purposes only. Every attempt has been made to provide accurate, up to date and reliable complete information. No warranties of any kind are expressed or implied. Readers acknowledge that the author is not engaging in the rendering of legal, financial, medical or professional advice. The content of this book has been derived from various sources. Please consult a licensed professional before attempting any techniques outlined in this book.

By reading this document, the reader agrees that under no circumstances are is the author responsible for any losses, direct or indirect, which are incurred as a result of the use of information contained within this document, including, but not limited to, —errors, omissions, or inaccuracies.

Table of Contents

Introduction 1
Chapter 1: What is Wicca Magic? 3
Chapter 2: Basic Wiccan Principles 7
Chapter 3: Wiccan Gods Explained 13
    Single God 13
    Two Gods 14
    Many Gods 14
    Love for Nature 14
    No God 15
    Indifferent 15
    The Concept of Divine Energy 16
Chapter 4: Setting up an Altar 23
    Altar 24
Chapter 5: Wicca Love Spells 29
    Finding True Love 29
    Spell for Sex 31
    Spell for Ideal Partner 33
Chapter 6: Wicca Luck Spells 35
    Simple Luck Spell 35
    New Year Lucky Spell 36
    Spell for a Job 38
    Confidence Spell 40

Chapter 7: Wicca Health Spells 43
- Healing Spell 43
- Anger Spell 44
- Good Sleep Spell 45
- Beauty Spell 46
- Alternate Beauty Spell 48
- Ridding Infection 49
- Magic Spell for Overall Good Health 50
- Clearing Negative Emotions 51
- Chakra Cleansing Spell 53

Chapter 8: Wicca Money Spells 55
- Spell for Increasing Money 55
- Alternate Spell 57
- Getting Rid of Debt 58

Chapter 9: Wicca Magic FAQs 61

Chapter 10: Different Elements of Wicca 65
- Earth 65
- Air 66
- Fire 67
- Water 68
- Spirit 69

Chapter 11: Precautions 71
- Follow to a T 71
- Free Will 72

- Gains 72
- Take it Slow 73
- Do Not Cast Negative Spells 73
- Choose Carefully 74
- Understand Power 74
- Partner 75
- Expectations 75
- Privacy 76
- Cleansing 76

Chapter 12: Cleansing Wiccan Tools and Instruments 77
- Herbs 77
- Sea Salt 78
- Crystals 78
- Sun 79
- Moon 79
- Mud Bath 79
- Blow 80
- Water 80

Conclusion 83

Introduction

Wicca can be termed as a new age religion that incorporates witchcraft. It came into existence during the early 20th century and has since grown. Gerald Gardner is widely regarded as the father of Wicca, having introduced the art to enthusiasts in 1954.

Wiccan rituals or Wicca magic are inspired by pagan rituals that existed in the early 16th century as well as certain priestly rituals from the 20th century.

These priests were better referred to as wizards thereby lending this form of magic the name "Wicca". It is white magic and has no relevance to black magic whatsoever. Wicca magic is quite flexible and does not follow rigid rules. It relies on certain basic principles that guide the religion and sticking to them successfully fosters Wicca ideologies. These beliefs or central principles were laid down in the late 1940s by Doreen Valiente and Gerald Gardner, and are treated as gospel by the Wiccan community.

Introduction

If you are keen on taking up this type of religion and use spells to enhance your life, then this book will serve as your extensive guide to Wicca magic.

The book has been designed to teach you the basics of Wicca magic. It will guide you through the steps to follow in order to adopt Wicca in your life.

Let us begin.

Chapter 1:
What is Wicca Magic?

Magic has existed for a long time. Magic refers to altering reality in order to attain desirable results. This, of course, is easier said than done, but not impossible. With the right type of approach, it is easy to adopt magic and put it to good use.

One such magic used to alter reality is Wicca magic. Wicca magic is more of a religion that involves using spells to attain everything that one desires. The word Wicca is derived from "wic" meaning to shape or bend. This stands for the fact that Wicca is used to shape or bend the reality and mold it to one's liking.

Wicca magic is regarded as a powerful yet secretive form of energy that a few people use to alter their realities and change the course of their destiny. They do so in order to attain their heart's desire and enhance their living. Wiccans consider magic to be their birthright and treat it as a way of life. It is not compared to magic that is performed to entertain

Chapter 1: What is Wicca Magic?

people. It has its own place and is a way of life for many that take it up seriously.

Regular magic tends to rely on manipulating other people and trying to mold their behavior. This is, however, is not a feature of Wicca magic, as it does not believe in altering other people's minds and actions. It tends to tell people that it is possible to bend things such as spoons. Wicca, however, does not promote any such beliefs; it focuses more on bending the situation and making it ideal.

It focuses on changing the environment that surrounds us and influencing it to attain the desired end result. Wicca also promotes nature worship and seeking the blessing of Mother Nature to attain one's desires.

By casting Wiccan spells, a person has the chance to change his or her reality, surroundings as also themselves. This is made possible through the application of the different rituals as prescribed by Wicca. Wicca magic uses certain principles as the basis for casting spells. Wicca is now quite popular around the world with both men and women taking it up to attain their needs. Although these spells are now quite widespread, they were originally designed to be passed down from master to student.

Wicca is a polytheist religion, which means that the followers worship many Gods and goddesses.

Of these, there are two prominent Gods as per Wiccan tradition namely the horned God and the moon Goddess. They follow pagan religion thereby offering many types of offerings to these gods.

The moon Goddess is generally referred to as the great Goddess and is always represented as embracing the horned god, better known as the great horned god. Wicca has changed over time but managed to hold on to its core principles. In fact, the art of Wicca magic has diversified in many ways and is now a full-fledged religion.

In the following chapter, we will review the basic principles of the religion. Reading through them will help you understand how it works and how to adopt it in your life.

Chapter 2:
Basic Wiccan Principles

Wicca follows certain basic principles that form the basis of the religion. Here is looking at them in detail.

1. Wicca is a nature-based religion, which means that nature's elements are considered supreme. A Wiccan becomes one with nature by following the phases of a moon and appeasing it. They perform a ritual to please the various phases and also the various seasons. Doing so regularly can help in attaining everything that one desires in life. Nature is all giving and

2. Wiccans are of the opinion that they are superior amongst people and that bestows upon them a supreme power. Worshipping nature and appeasing its elements acquire this power. But the power needs to be used wisely by maintaining natural balance. It is important to showcase love to animals and birds and preserve their natural

surroundings. This is only possible through careful evaluation of the surroundings and picking the right spot to perform the rituals.

3. Although Wiccans consider themselves as being a little more powerful than regular people, this is only because they tap into their hidden power. This power is present inside each and every person, but not all make an effort to mold it. So it is not any extra power that they are blessed with but rather materializing what is hidden within.

4. Wiccans believe that there is no superior power when it comes to males and females and that both need to be worshipped equally. This is why both the God and Goddess are worshipped together and not separated. They work in unison with each other to bestow the worshipper with all that he desires. They consider sex to be a way of uniting the bodies as also unifying two divine elements.

5. Wicca magicians are constantly aware of their inner and outer limits. They know to look internally and externally. They consider all the elements that lie within them and outside of them and look for the paranormal that exists between the two. Failing to take both

into consideration will not help a Wiccan come face to face with the ultimate power.

6. Wiccans do not believe in superiority within their circle. This means that a teacher is no different or higher in power than a student and they both lie on the same plane. The student will always respect the teacher but not be under their influence. There is, however, a special place in the religion for all those that take on the onus of educating others about the religion and how it can be adopted.

7. Wicca magic is not forced upon anyone and is adopted through free will. This is an important aspect of the religion and one that helps in keeping a person interested for life. The person is made to look at the world as a magical place where all individuals are free to choose what they wish to do without being forced into something. This promotes harmony and established peace within the Wiccan community.

8. The Wiccan community does not believe in lending titles and name-calling. Although most practitioners are referred to as witches and wizards, these are not titles that they swear by. None of these titles are passed

Chapter 2: Basic Wiccan Principles

down from generation to generation, and a Wiccan earns the title by himself. The highest titles will only come about through regular and dedicated practice.

9. All Wiccans believe that they have been chosen to carry forward the legacy of the religion. They are meant to strengthen the Wiccan beliefs and pass it on to others. Each one has their role defined and will make all efforts to honor the principles that guide Wiccan religion. They are free to choose the means in which they propagate the message.

10. Wiccans are extremely peace loving. They do not indulge in activities that bring down or tarnish other religions such as Christianity. It is just a misconception that Wiccans condemn all other religions. In fact, they are welcoming of other people who would like to maintain their religion and yet take up Wicca magic to influence their life.

11. Many people have questioned the basis of Wiccan religion and wondered if it is genuine. This, however, does not bother the Wiccan community, as they are not affected by false claims. They do not wish to delve into the origins of the practice and wish to focus on the current state.

12. Contrary to popular belief, the Wiccans do not indulge in any form of devil worship. There is widespread misconception that Wiccans worship Satan in order to avail his favor. But this is not true. The only God they worship is the horned god, who can be mistaken to be the devil owing to the presence of horns. But these Gods are not related to any form of Satanism. Wiccans do not indulge in any form of evil practice that can harm others. They only aim at fulfilling their own wishes and desires by summoning the gods.

13. Nature is every Wiccan's biggest inspiration. They turn to it for all their physical and mental needs. They believe that nature is the ultimate giver of happiness. Wiccans believe that they will one day become one with the Earth and strive hard to keep her happy.

These core principles guide Wiccan religion. It is important for all new Wiccans to understand and follow them in order to switch to the religion with ease. Here is looking at a basic mindset to posses while casting spells. It is important for you to possess a positive mind while casting the spells. Ensure that you invest complete faith in Wicca in order to reap its full benefits. If you remain skeptical, then you might not see positive results.

Chapter 2: Basic Wiccan Principles

It will be important for you to keep your practice a secret. This is especially important after casting a spell. Do not tell anybody about it and keep it a secret. Try to keep away from negativity as much as possible. There will always be some people who will look down upon you and your practice. Do not encourage or entertain them and learn to ignore them.

Be patient and wait for a spell to work before casting another. Casting too many at once can get confusing and might not produce the results that you would want.

Chapter 3:
Wiccan Gods Explained

Wiccan is a pagan religion. This means that its followers worship Gods and goddesses. Here is looking at some of the definitions as per Wicca religion.

Single God

Monotheism is a concept that pertains to worshipping one God or Goddess. It is one where a person worships just one God that he thinks is superior to the others. Some Wiccans prefer to be monotheists as it helps them appease their God in a better manner. A Wiccan can pick who he wants to worship. The God can be the horned God or Cernunnos and the Goddess can be the mother. Some believe that it is not possible to separate the two and are more or less fused together. The horned God is known as Mal and the Goddess is known as the mother. Since there are more numbers of female wiccans, the Goddess remains quite popular amongst the two.

Chapter 3: Wiccan Gods Explained

Two Gods

Duotheism refers to worshipping two Gods or rather a male and female god. Both are worshipped separately and not fused together. The male God stands for masculinity and everything male. The Goddess represents femininity and all the elements attached to the female aspect of life. The two are not combined and worshipped as different entities. Many Wiccans are duotheists and prefer to worship the horned God and the Goddess separately.

Many Gods

Polytheism refers to worshipping several different Gods and Goddess. Religions such as Hinduism follow this type of system where many Gods exist. Some Wiccans are polytheists as they worship many different Gods and goddesses. Apart from the horned God and mother goddess, there are many other Gods as per the Wiccan religion that the followers worship. We will look at some of them in the following segment.

Love for Nature

Pantheism refers to nature worship. Many Wiccans consider nature to be the ultimate giver. All Wiccans develop a deep and strong connection with nature, as they consider it to be their ultimate god. Wiccans wish to protect nature and worship responsibly. They strive to protect all the elements in nature; right from trees to plants to the sun to the moon, everything is considered precious and worshipped.

No God

It is interesting to note that within the Wiccan community lie some atheists. They do not believe in worshipping any God or Goddess. They will perform the different Wiccan rituals without summoning any divine entity. This is possible as there is no set rules when it comes to picking Gods and goddesses as per the wiccan religion and everybody is free to do what they think is best for them, as long as it remains within the 13 principles set down.

Indifferent

The last type is agnostic. This type refers to those that do not believe in religion of any kind. They treat Wicca as a means to attain their goals and do not believe in Gods and goddesses. Agnostics will not indulge in setting up altars and performing the rituals. They will instead simply follow the basic principles mentioned as per the religion.

Chapter 3: Wiccan Gods Explained

These form the different categories to choose from. It is entirely up to you to choose whatever you think will work well for you. It will help to do some research on these and know exactly what will be in store for you.

The Concept of Divine Energy

Wiccans are of the opinion that ultimate energy can be attained through the fusion of the God and the Goddess. They balance each other out in order to produce energy. It follows the path of yin and yang, which is a Chinese concept that stresses on the fusion of male and female energy.

Here is looking closely at the God and the Goddess that Wiccans worship.

The God

The God is better known as the masculine energy. He represents masculinity and is worshipped for his immense power. He is generally depicted as having two horns and a long beard. Many Wiccans consider him to be the God of animals with the horns representing antlers. Some critics are of the opinion that it signifies the devil, but this is just a misconception, as the God does not represent anything evil. In fact, it showcases virility and tells us how powerfully profound the God really is.

As mentioned earlier, Wiccans worship nature. They are of the opinion that nature is the ultimate God and therefore the horned God is sometimes represented as a tree with his body branching out. He is depicted as being green and embracing the Goddess. Oak and holly are both worshipped by Wiccans and it is believed that the horned God represents both. Many people worship large trees as they consider it to be their god.

The God has many names including Cernunnos, Kernunno and Pan. Each Wiccan has a different name for him but is mostly only referred to as the horned god.

The horned God is said to be a passionate over. The Wiccans look at sex as a means to connect the mind and body. Many of the rituals that they follow involve using sex as a medium to connect with the god.

You are free to use both idols and pictures of the God and incorporate it in your daily worship.

The Goddess

The Goddess represents femininity. She stands for all things feminine and balances the masculine aspect. The Goddess is generally depicted with a crescent on her head and a long flowy white gown. She is the epitome of beauty and looks divine. She is

Chapter 3: Wiccan Gods Explained

always shown as embracing the horned god, while the two unite together to create balance and harmony. The Goddess is generally represented as three different women including the mother, the crone and the maiden. All three are extremely powerful and capable of pleasing her worshippers.

She is extremely knowledgeable and therefore represented as the crone. Many Wiccans know her by the name of Diana and consider her to be the moon. She smoothly transitions from one phase to another while embracing her subjects.

Those that worship the Goddess also worship the moon and its different phases. They tend to perform a different ritual to appease the varying phases of the moon.

Many are of the opinion that the God and Goddess are a single entity. They are embodied differently but contain the same spirit. This makes it easier for them to choose either one and worship him or her.

They will both work together to help the worshipper attain all that he or she desire.

Here is looking at the different Gods that are worshipped.

- **Adonis** – The God of agriculture and rebirth, this Greek God is called upon to bless the worshipper with constant supply of food.

- **Apollo** – Apollo is the God of music and poetry and is called upon to enhance their artistic side.

- **Anubis** – Anubis is an Egyptian God who is said to take care of the dead. Some Wiccans call upon him to safeguard the souls of people that have passed away.

- **Aten** – Aten is the Greek God of sun who is called upon to attain power and promote positivity.

- **Brahma** – Brahma is a Hindu God also known as the creator of the universe. He is summoned to create something special.

- **Cernunnos** – Cernunnos is the horned God worshipped by the wiccans. He is masculine and worshipped for his power.

- **Dagda** – Dagda is and Irish God who is summoned to provide relief in a serious situation.

Chapter 3: Wiccan Gods Explained

- **Dionysus** – He is the Greek God of music and love and is summoned to influence both of these aspects.

- **Eros** – he is the God of sexuality and love and is summoned to enhance both of these aspects of life.

- **Ganesha** – He is the famous Indian God who is summoned to remove obstacles that lie in the way.

- **Krishna** – Krishna is a Hindu God summoned to promote balance and enhance positivity.

- **Holly King** – Holly king is summoned to establish peace.

- **Horus** – Horus is summoned before the beginning of a new task.

- **Lugh** – Lugh is summoned to enhance productivity.

- **Mercury** – Mercury is summoned to avail a safe journey.

- **Oak King** – this God is called upon to enhance business and increase profits.

- **Odin** – Odin is the God of wisdom and intelligence and summoned to enhance the same.

- **Pan** – Pan is summoned to promote new life.

- **Ra** – Ra is an Egyptian God who is summoned to enhance positivity.

- **Shiva** – Shiva is a Hindu God known to destroy negativity. He is summoned to keep negative energy at bay.

- **Sunna** – Sunna is a Norse God who is summoned to maintain peace.

- **Thoth** – Those that wish to enhance their intelligence summon Thoth, who is the God of wisdom.

- **Vishnu** – Vishnu is a Hindu God summoned to sustain positivity and increase its effects on a person's life.

These are the different Gods that can be invoked when you wish to achieve something through Wicca magick.

Chapter 4:
Setting up an Altar

Wicca magic is all about appeasing Gods and casting spells. These spells are cast using a book of shadows. The book of shadows is a personal book containing the spells that you wish to cast. There is no such gospel book available that can be bought from a store and should be crafted personally. The name is suggestive of a book straight out of a harry potter movie but there is actually nothing too fancy.

It will take time for you to craft such a book and must remain patient. You have to fill in details about your Wiccan practice and the spells that you wish to cast. This book will leave you with many spells that can be cast to attain your desires. You have the choice to pick the type of book to fill. A physical one works better than a virtual one, as you will have a physical copy of it.

What you wish to write in your book and how you want to structure it is up to you. You can write about the Gods and goddesses you wish to worship. Write

Chapter 4: Setting up an Altar

spells; write about your experiences, your wants and desires etc. Once you fill in the details, place the book on a bookstand. The bookstand will be placed on the altar where you place the rest of the elements. You have to ensure you read through the book every day or alternate day, as it will help you connect better with it.

Altar

It is very important to set up an altar before you begin your pagan practice. The altar is where you keep all your books, tools, idols and the like. The altar should be located in a sacred place, as it will be considered a sacrosanct. It will be the place where you will cast your spells. If you are unable to dedicate a permanent place to your altar then it is also an option to use a make shift one.

It is best to find a flat surface to set up the altar. You will have enough space to arrange everything and use it for the rituals. Make sure the surface is clean and free from dust and dirt. It can be a table, a shelf or a makeshift stool.

If you are a believer in feng shui then look up the best direction or location to set up the altar as that can further boost the results of the practice.

As mentioned earlier, Wiccans respect privacy and ensure that they perform the rituals secretively. It would therefore be best to set up the altar in a place where only you have access. This will ensure that others are not disturbed.

Tools and equipment

Here is a look at the different elements that will go on the altar.

- God/ goddess

You have the choice to pick any deity that you would like to sit on the altar. We had a look at the different Gods to consider and can choose any one of them. You may also choose multiple Gods but will get a bit cumbersome. Once you pick the right God or Goddess you have to buy a statue or memento to represent him or her. If there is no place to keep an idol then a photograph will also do.

- A ritual knife known as Athame

The Athame is a sword or knife that is placed on the altar. It is a traditional blade with steel blade and black handle. If in case you are unable to find a metal blade then a wooden one will also work just as well.

Chapter 4: Setting up an Altar

- Bells

Bells are a big part of Wiccan rituals. The bell is used to garner the chosen deity's attention before commencing the ritual. The sound of the bell also awakens your senses and makes you alert. Shake the bell before buying it to check the quality of jingle.

- Candles

As you know, candles are a big part of most traditions. A candle represents fire, which is an important element to incorporate into your rituals. Buy any candle you like and place them in front of the deity. Apart from these you will also need different colored candles to perform the different rituals.

- Salt

Salt is an important part of Wiccan rituals. A bowl of salt or Earth should be placed on the altar to represent nature. Try to use a ceramic bowl and fill it up with sea salt or red soil.

- Chalice

The chalice is used to represent the Goddess. It signifies femininity and is meant to enhance positivity. The chalice is generally made of white metal such as silver but can pick any metal you like.

- Pentacle

The pentacle is symbolic of Wicca traditions and rituals. It is used to decorate the altar and appease the gods. It is a circle with a star in the center. Either draw it or use a cut out to place on the altar.

- Wand

No Wicca practice is complete without a wand. It can be made of wood or metal. Buy a sturdy one that can be used several times. Place it in front of the bookstand or on top of it.

- Cauldron

A cauldron is an optional element to have on your altar. It is used to place incense sticks and other such elements. Buy a small one and place it on the altar.

- Crystals

Certain crystals have powers that can be used to enhance spells. These can be placed on the altar to avail full benefits.

- Duster

Keep a duster or broom handy to clean the altar from time to time.

Chapter 4: Setting up an Altar

Remember to pick the items that suit you best. They should be a representation of you on the altar. Some people like to keep it simple and clean and avoid clutter while some use a large altar to incorporate all of the different elements.

There are many specialty stores where you can buy these. But if you are unable to do so then they can also be ordered online.

Refrain from buying used tools as they will carry with them a certain level of negativity. You might not be able to avail ideal results by using used tools and equipment. If you are on a strict budget then pick only some of the important tools from the list.

As mentioned earlier, you have the choice of a makeshift altar. Keep all the elements in a box and carry it to wherever you wish to set up the altar.

Chapter 5:
Wicca Love Spells

Here is looking at simple Wicca spells to try out to enhance your everyday life.

Love is one of the most important elements of life. Here are simple spells to enhance your love and sex life.

Finding True Love

Finding true love is one of the toughest things in life but not an impossible task. Here is looking at a simple spell that can be cast to find true, everlasting love.

It is important to follow the different rituals meant to enhance each spell. For this, you must perform them on the designated day and wear appropriately colored clothing.

This particular spell should be performed on Friday nights only and it is best to wear the color red while performing it.

Chapter 5: Wicca Love Spells

Things required

- 1 red waterproof marker
- 1 sheet of white paper
- 1 white envelope
- 2-3 drops of essential oil
- Lipstick of your choice
- 6 fresh red rose petals

Method

- Start by making a list of what you want your true love to be like.
- You will want him or her to possess certain qualities that make them perfect.
- Use the marker and write down the qualities on the piece of paper.
- Remember to keep it real and don't have too many far-fetched expectations.
- Fold the paper and place it in the envelope.
- Use the essential oil to seal the envelope.

- Apply the lipstick and kiss the envelope (men can skip this).

- Place it on the altar and sprinkle the rose petals on top. Summon the Gods and envision the person of your dreams.

- Let the envelope remain there until you find your partner and not open it. Once you find him or her, destroy the envelope without opening it.

Spell for Sex

This spell is for all those that wish to enhance their sex life and improve their love life as a whole.

Things required

- 1 garnet crystal
- Some fresh pink rose petals
- Red wine in a goblet or chalice
- Bowl of Earth

Chapter 5: Wicca Love Spells

Method

- Sit in front of the altar and draw a circle around you.

- Summon the moon Goddess and feel her presence.

- Sprinkle the rose petals in front of you and place the bowl of Earth on top of it.

- Hold the garnet in your hand and close your eyes. Visualize your sexual fantasies and the person you want to have it with.

- Place the garnet in the center of the bowl and pour the wine over it.

- While doing so envision the person you wish to have the experience with.

- This should be a partner or someone that is already in a relationship with you.

- This spell might not work if you envision someone that is not interested in you.

- Once done, pick up the bowl and empty it in a special place close to your heart like your garden.

Spell for Ideal Partner

An ideal person need not always be your lover. Summon the Gods to grant you a caring person capable of taking care of you.

Here is a spell to find the right life partner and start a romantic relationship with him or her.

Things required

- Candle holders
- 1 red or pink candle
- 1 white candle
- Pink chalk
- Pink or red cloth

Method

- Clean and clear away the altar. Sit in front of it and hold the candle in your hand. Now close your eyes and envision the person you wish to be your lover.

- Speak out the characteristics that you wish to seek in him or her. Again, keep it realistic and something that can be expected of a person.

Chapter 5: Wicca Love Spells

- Place the candle next to you and spread the cloth on the altar. Add the candleholders on the cloth and use the chalk to draw a heart in between them. Color in the heart completely if you like. Place the white candle on the right and the pink candle on the left.

- Leave everything as it is. Every evening, sit in the same place and light both the candles. Chant the qualities that you seek in the person you wish to pursue. Say them out loudly after summoning the God or Goddess of choice.

- Do so every day until you find the right one. If you wish to make it just a one week spell then move the candles an inch closer every day for 1 week and stop when they touch other.

- Once they close in summon the Goddess Aphrodite and call upon her to bless you with the ideal partner of choice. Once done, light up the candles and allow them to completely burn out.

- Remain patient while the spell works its magic on you.

Chapter 6:
Wicca Luck Spells

Simple Luck Spell

Ingredients

- 1 black candle
- Essential oil of your choice (preferably herb oil)

Method

- Place the candle on the altar and sit in front of it.
- Put some of the oil on your fingertips and run it over the candle.
- Stare at it and chant

"Black candle, turn my luck around Bring prosperity and joy abound"

- Now light the candle and close your eyes for a minute.

Chapter 6: Wicca Luck Spells

- Open it and stare at the flame while chanting

"Flame and fire, candle burn Work to make my luck return"

- Now visualize yourself as the luckiest person on Earth.
- Everything you ever desired is coming your way.
- Allow the candle to burn down completely.
- Repeat 2 to 3 times a week.

New Year Lucky Spell

Things required

- Pen and paper
- Incense sticks
- Black candle
- Chalice
- Bowl of water
- Quartz crystal small jar

Method

- Calm yourself down and sit at the altar.

- Now neatly write down all that you wish to come your way during New Year.

- Now light the candle and incense sticks.

- Place the paper under the candle and chant

"God and Goddess, Mother and Father I give my thanks for all that I have With air I cleanse the past To prepare for a prosperous new year For the highest good So be it"

- Now add the water to the chalice and place it in front of you.

- Chant

"God and Goddess, Mother and Father I give my thanks for all that I have With water I vitalize the future To prepare for a prosperous new year For the highest good So be it"

- Drink the water and close your eyes.

- This spell can be performed every new year.

Chapter 6: Wicca Luck Spells

Spell for a Job

Here is a simple spell that can be used to land your dream job.

Things required

- A recent photo of yourself
- 3 to 4 Green candles
- Essential oil of your choice
- Incense sticks
- 10 fresh bay leaves
- 2 green fluorite stones
- Money bill
- Ceramic bowl

Method

- Wear white clothes while performing this ritual.
- Apply a few drops of the essential oil on your wrists and rub them together.
- Start by making a circle around you and place the candles in front.

- Burn the incense sticks next to it.
- Now place your photo in front of the candle.
- Light up the candles and drop a few drops of wax on your photo.
- Hold the ceramic bowl in your hand and place the stones in it.
- Chant

"Success is coming soon to me, Prosperity is flowing unto me, so mote it be"

- Close your eyes and visualize yourself as having attained financial freedom and landing the dream job.
- Drown yourself in the feeling and feel the thrill.
- Once done, blow out the candles.
- Repeat this until you land the job of your dreams.

Chapter 6: Wicca Luck Spells

Confidence Spell

Things required

- 1 golden candle
- Tiger's eye
- Sandalwood essential oil

Method

- Wear red or orange clothes while performing this ritual.
- Place everything on the altar.
- Close your eyes and visualize yourself as a confident person.
- Remove every possible doubt from your mind and prepare yourself mentally.
- Draw a circle around yourself.
- Hold the golden candle in your hand and apply some drops of sandalwood oil on it.
- Chant

I call upon the energies of the Sun and the Earth,

To help me find my confidence and self-worth

- Now place the candle in front of you and light it.

- Place the tiger's eye in the cup and hold it in your hand.

- Now focus on the flame and imagine a ball of divine light emerging from you.

- Close your eyes and make it as vivid as possible.

- Imagine this light to be the love and blessing of Gods above you.

- Visualize the horned God and moon Goddess smiling down on you and expanding your aura.

- You are the most confident person on earth.

- Feel this love coming your way and opening up your mind.

- All your inhibitions have left you.

- Once done, slowly open up your fingers and feel the crystal absorbing all the positive energy.

Chapter 6: Wicca Luck Spells

- Keep this crystal with you everywhere that you go. It will promote confidence and help you feel blessed.

Chapter 7:
Wicca Health Spells

Healing Spell

This spell is cast to heal the body and mind. It is cast to help the body heal from a condition and develop resistance.

It is easy to cast and will leave you with good results. Here is how to cast the healing spell.

Things required

- Bowl of soup of your choice (preferably chicken as it has healing powers)
- 1 candle
- 2 drops clove essential oil

Method

- Apply drops of the oil on your wrists and rub together.
- Place the candle in front and light it.

Chapter 7: Wicca Health spells

- Place the bowl of soup next to it and chant

"Apollo, God of Healing
I call upon the assistance of thee
Bless this soup with the powers to heal
Apollo, God of Healing please assist me"

- Close your eyes and visualize yourself healing.

- Blow at the candle to diffuse it.

- Now slowly eat the soup and visualize it travelling through your body and healing you.

- Once done, take rest.

- Repeat this until you are healed.

Anger Spell

Anger can be devastating and impact you negatively. Here is a simple spell that can aid in banishing anger.

Things required

- A stone or crystal of your choice

Method

- Hold the stone or crystal in your palm and close your eyes.

- Visualize all your negative feelings disappearing.

- Clutch it as tightly as you feel all your anger going away.

- Once done, visualize yourself as a calmer person.

- Let all the negativity go away and start meditating.

Good Sleep Spell

Things required

- 1 small smoky quartz
- Small piece of paper
- Pen

Method

- This spell should be performed on the bed before falling asleep.

Chapter 7: Wicca Health spells

- Sleep on the bed and hold the quartz in your hand.

- Close your eyes and visualize any ill and bad feelings that are affecting you.

- Now place the stone to the side and write down all that is negatively impacting you.

- Wrap the paper around the stone and place it under your pillow.

- Sleep over it.

- The next morning tear the paper into small bits and discard it or simply burn it.

- Do this for two other nights and make sure you dispose off the paper.

- This will help you avail better sleep.

Beauty Spell

Beauty spells are cast to appear more attractive and appeal to others. Here is a simple spell that can do the trick for you.

Things required

- Pink candles

- Pink rose petals
- Rose and lavender essential oils
- Incense of your choice
- Bath tub

Method

- To perform this spell start by filling up the tub with warm water. Add in the drops of rose and lavender oil and mix well. Place the candles and incense on the tub and burn them.

- Sprinkle the rose petals and sit inside. Close your eyes and chant

**"Earth, Air, Fire, Sea,
Let the Goddess' Beauty shine through me!**

- Repeat this as many times as possible. If you do not have a bathtub then this can also be followed in the shower.

- Repeat for a week.

Chapter 7: Wicca Health spells

Alternate Beauty Spell

Here is a simple alternate beauty spell for you to try out.

Things required

- A red apple
- A sharp knife

Method

- Place the apple on the altar and sit in front of it.
- Wear white clothes for this ritual.
- Now chant

Apple, sacred fruit of the Goddess, with this gift, I do caress the pimple that brought me shame. I banish this zit in your name

- Pick up the apple and rub it over your face.
- Chant

I love and accept myself as I am today. Clear skin I summon to come my way. By My Will so Mote It Be Three times three times three.

- Pick up the other half of the fruit and bury it in the garden.

- Throw the used half into a water body.

- Repeat until your issue is resolved.

Ridding Infection

This is a simple spell that can be cast to get rid of any bacterial infections.

Things required

- White candle

- Bay leaf oil

Method

- Sprinkle some of the oil over the candle and allow it to sit.

- Burn the candle and stare at the flame.

- Now visualize the flame as travelling to your wound and destroying all the bacteria there.

- Allow the flame to stay there and then leave as the bacteria fades away.

- Repeat this until your wound heals.

Chapter 7: Wicca Health spells

"Abracadabra" is one of the most popular words used in the history of Magick, Wiccan or otherwise! The word "Abracadabra" is said to be derived from an Aramaic phrase which means "I create like the word". It is believed that the word has healing properties when it is inscribed on an amulet.

Magic Spell for Overall Good Health

This is a simple spell that will promote good health.

Things required

- Piece of paper
- Pen

Method

Start by writing the word Good Health on a piece of paper.

Now keep writing the same by cutting out the last alphabet in the word, which is as follows.

Good Health
Good Healt
Good Heal
Good Hea
Good He
Good H

Good
Goo
Go
G

- Now roll up the scroll as tightly as possible.

- Now place it inside a locket or pendant and wear it around your neck.

- Keep it on until your illness goes away.

Clearing Negative Emotions

Things required

- 1 candle

- Bowl of water

- Bowl of earth

- Herbs such as sage and rosemary

- Ceramic bowl

Method

- Start by clearing the altar and place everything over it.

- Burn the candle in front of you.

Chapter 7: Wicca Health spells

- Now draw a circle around you and chant

I call upon the Elements in this simple ceremony that I may be cleansed from the contamination of negativity.

- Gently wave your hand over the flame and chant

I willingly release negative action in my fire.

- Now rub some of the soil over your hands and chant

I release stumbling blocks and obstacles in my earth.

- Now add the chosen herbs to the bowl and set it on fire.

- Allow it to burn and produce smoke.

- Wave the smoke in front of you by moving the bowl and chant

I clear my air of unwise thoughts.

- Next, dip your fingers in the bowl of water and chant

I purify this water. Let this relinquishing be gentle. Purified, cleansed and released in all

ways, I now acknowledge my trust and faith in my own clarity.

- Once done, visualize yourself as a calmer person and let go of all your ill and negative feelings.

- When you finish with the ritual throw the soil into the garden and do the same with the water.

Chakra Cleansing Spell

Chakras are an important part of the body. They help in keeping the related organs healthy. Here is how to cleanse them.

Things required

- 1 tablespoon red rose petals
- 1 tablespoon orange peel
- 1 tablespoon chamomile flowers
- 1 tablespoon tulips
- 1 tablespoon lavender flowers
- 2 tablespoons salt

Chapter 7: Wicca Health spells

Method

- Mix all of these together and give it a good shake.

- Add it to the bathtub and fill with water.

- Sit in the tub and concentrate on these elements cleansing each and every chakra in your body.

- Repeat this 2 to 3 times a week.

Chapter 8:
Wicca Money Spells

Who doesn't want to be rich? Everybody in this world strives to make more money and lead the life of his or her dreams.

Although there is no substitute for hard work, there is also the choice to cast a spell.

It will be important to keep it real but nothing is above Wicca magic. Here is looking at simple spells to cast.

Spell for Increasing Money

This is a simple spell to increase the money in your life. It is easy to cast and will help you remain with more money.

Things required

- Small piece of paper
- Bay leaf or geranium essential oil

Chapter 8: Wicca Money Spells

- 1 Green Candle

- Incense sticks of your choice

Method

- Use a green color marker to draw a dollar on the paper. Vary the color of the marker depending on the color of your local currency. Fill it in completely and make it realistic.

- Place it in front on the altar and sit in front of it. Summon the God of money and close your eyes while chanting his name.

- Now sprinkle some of the essential oil on the candle and place it in front of you on the altar. Fold the drawing and place it below the candle in front of you.

- Light the candle and incense sticks and place them side-by-side. Concentrate on the flame of the candle and chant the following

God and Goddess hear my call,
Please make money come my way,
Help me gain money

- Focus on the dollar bill as you chant this spell. Visualize more money flowing into your account and the number of bundles multiplying.

- Do this everyday for at least 7 days at a stretch. After seven days pick out the paper and burn it away.

- Allow it to burn away completely and visualize the money multiplying.

Alternate Spell

This is an alternate spell to increase your money. This is slightly easier than the previous one and can leave you with similar results.

Things required

- Any coin

- A houseplant

- A little sage herb

Chapter 8: Wicca Money Spells

Method

- Take care of your plant once you bring it home and allow it to blossom for a week. Place it in front of you on the altar. Pick some of the herb and rub between your fingers. Now sprinkle it over the plant.

- Place the coin on the soil and push it inwards. Make sure you don't fully bury it and keep some of it on top.

- Now, whenever you come into money, pick this coin up and spend it on something you like. Replace it with another coin and spend that when you come into money again and so on and so forth.

- Keep this going until you are happy with the money you have.

Getting Rid of Debt

Debt is one of the most dreaded aspects of life. Here is looking at a spell to cast to get rid of all your existing debts.

Things required

- 1 red marker

- A piece of paper
- A white candle
- Ylang ylang essential oil

Method

- Start by writing down all the debts that you have. Make sure you do not leave out anything.
- Now sit in front of the altar and place the candle in front. Fold the paper and place it below the candle. Sprinkle the essential oil on the candle and burn it.
- Close your eyes and visualize all your debt being repaid. While you do so chant the following
- May all my debt disappear
- Repeat this for a week and then burn away the envelope. Visualize all of your debt paid off.

Chapter 9:
Wicca Magic FAQs

Wicca magic is pretty straightforward but you might have a few questions about it. Here is looking at some.

Is Wicca a bona fide practice?

Wicca is quite a genuine art but just like real magic it does not have scientific backing. Wicca can be used to alter destiny and avail positive benefits. Regular practice will ensure you attain all that you desire in life.

Is it safe to practice Wicca magic?

Yes it is safe to practice Wicca magic. Casting positive spells will help you attain your desires. The practice does not promote the use of negative spells so there is no need to worry about any negative effects or side effects as such.

Chapter 9: Wicca Magic FAQs

Can there be negative effects?

Wicca magic does not promote the casting of negative spells. If you indulge in it then you might have to bear the consequences. But if you steer clear of any such negativity then you can easily avoid any negative effects.

Is it ideal for everybody?

Anybody who wishes to use Wicca magic to enhance his or her life can take it up. It is open to all and does not impose any restrictions or compulsions. Both men and women can adopt it. But it is best to understand what Wicca has in store for you before taking it up.

How fast do results show?

Results will depend on how much effort you have put in casting the spells. Using good quality tools and casting powerful spells will help you avail faster results. You must put in positive energy in order to remain with positive results. Try to be as patient as possible and the results will slowly flow in.

Can I discontinue when i like?

Yes, you may discontinue practice when you like. But once you take up the religion it will be best to continue with it for a lifetime.

Can a spell be cast for another person?

If you are casting the spell to help another person avail positive results then you may do so. But it is best for individuals to cast their own spells. Wicca works best for those that first convert to the religion and then take it up.

These form the different questions regarding Wicca and hope you had yours answers.

Chapter 10:
Different Elements of Wicca

Wicca tradition includes 5 main elements. Here is looking at them in detail.

Earth

The most important element as per Wiccan culture is Earth. All of us are connected to Earth and will one day return to it. It is the densest element and made up of natural elements such as sand, rocks and trees.

Earth is considered as our mother who should be respected and worshipped. She represents femininity, creativity, practicality and passion.

Earth is connected to aspects such as wealth, money and prosperity. It is also related to responsibility and being grounded.

Chapter 10: Different Elements of Wicca

All the elements are governed by a particular season and direction. Earth is governed by winter with North being the direction.

The element of Earth is strongest in places where people meet such as the living room. It is also strongest where nature is present in abundance such as the garden area. It is a good idea to incorporate a little nature in your living room such as placing a plant in a corner.

As per Wiccan traditions, Gaia, who happens to be the moon goddess, represents Earth. Worshipping her will help in channelizing this element and seeking its favor. You will have the chance to attain more in life in terms of wealth and prosperity.

Air

Air is the next most important element as per Wiccan tradition. Air is invisible and the only element to have this quality. It is one of the most important elements on Earth as people depend on it to survive. Air, in fact, nourishes life and helps in cleansing our systems.

Air is governed by the East and concerned with spring. Air deals with rationality and making the right choices. It will be best to base this element in the Eastern direction.

It is also concerned mental well being and how a person conducts himself. Drawing in deep breaths can help in opening up the mind and enhance thinking capacity.

Air projects masculinity and clear thinking. It also promotes intelligence and communication. Those that appease this element have the chance to lead a life filled with clear thoughts.

Gods such as Mercury and Shu are worshipped in order to appease this element. Doing so also helps in increasing knowledge and enhancing thinking capacity. It also enhances wit and creativity.

People who are blessed by this element will excel at judging. They will be able to assess the situation and make the right decisions.

Fire

The next element is fire. It is also considered the fiercest of all elements, as it can be quite unpredictable.

It is both tough to create and control fire. If someone is trying to appease this particular element then it is best to be a little careful with it as not doing so can cause it to destroy all that lies in its path.

Chapter 10: Different Elements of Wicca

Fire is governed by the southern direction and pertains to summer. It will therefore be best to incorporate this element in the southern direction of your house.

Fire promotes creativity and ignites passion. Appeasing it can help in enhancing both these aspects and improving overall life.

But as mentioned earlier, it is important to handle this aspect carefully. If you fail to do so then you might have to deal with issues such as anger, egotism and other such aspects.

Summoning Gods such as Apollo and Lugh can influence this element. They help with enhancing passion and increase a person's creative capacity.

It is ideal for people who wish to enhance their personality and make it a bit more dazzling. Appeasing this element can also help with drawing out your inner spark.

Water

Water is the next element as per Wiccan religion. Water is fluid and therefore enhances life's fluidity.

Appeasing this element can help with increasing a person's thought process and make it fluid. Water also has a healing capacity on the mind and body of people.

It is governed by autumn and influenced by the west. It will therefore be ideal to incorporate this element in the western direction.

The Gods that are summoned to influence this element include Epona and Venus, who are extremely powerful. Calling unto them can help in enhancing good health and increasing positivity. It also helps in bettering relationships.

People who travel by sea regularly can summon these Gods in order to experience a smooth sailing journey.

Spirit

The last element that is worshipped is the spirit. The spirit refers to an invisible entity that exists in mysterious conditions.

Spirit, also known as ether, is connected with fine arts and the process of healing. It is quite tough to understand this aspect and tougher to appease it.

It is best for experienced people to invoke this element. It will be important to control it as otherwise it can go a bit out of control.

Chapter 10: Different Elements of Wicca

However, this element can be extremely giving once it is successfully tamed. It can help in enhancing all three vital elements of the body including soul, mind and body. It unifies the three and makes it possible for people to experience better living.

People will find it easy to experience a form of higher consciousness. It alters the 7th chakra in the body that is associated with intelligence and spirituality.

This element is associated with the colors white and black. Either can be draped while summoning this element.

These are the 5 main elements of Wiccan tradition. It will be important for you to understand their power and use them to your advantage.

Chapter 11:
Precautions

It is obvious that you will have to be a little careful with Wicca magic, as it is quite powerful.

Here is looking at certain aspects to bear in mind while taking up the practice.

Follow to a T

It will be quite important for you to follow the different rituals to a T. Go through the different spells again and see the correct order to be followed. It is quite important for you to cleanse yourself before a ritual and will make for an important part of the process. Try to use organic elements, as they will give you better results. Try growing your own herbs so that you will have a constant supply. It is also essential to follow the different procedures step by step as they are mentioned.

Chapter 11: Precautions

Free Will

Remember that Wicca magic does not promote negativity. This means that you cannot use it to influence others in any manner. Many people assume they have the power to change other people and get them to like or love them. But this is not possible without the other person willingly wanting to do it. It will be best to stick to personal gains such as inviting good luck and increasing monetary gains. But if you think someone might be interested in you and wish to help the relationship grow then cast a spell for the same.

Gains

It is possible for you to cast positive spells for others. They need not always be for you; they can also be cast for other people. Helping others will in turn help you. It will bring you luck and blessings. It is believed within the Wiccan community that you may avail 3 times the benefits. So if your spell works for someone else then you will be rewarded 3 times for it. On the flipside, if you cast a negative spell then you will have to bear thrice the consequences for it.

Take it Slow

It will pay to take things a little slow and not rush into anything. Wicca is extremely welcoming but requires a careful approach. Read as much as possible on the topic in order to better understand it. Read from different sources in order to get a good idea of what the culture is all about. Also go through this book again to pick up on the finer points. Once you get started with it, cast simple spells and check how they work for you before moving to some of the complex ones.

Do Not Cast Negative Spells

It is extremely important to cast positive spells and avoid negative ones. It is extremely important to steer clear of those spells that can turn out to harm others. It is important to keep birds and animals in mind before doing anything including casting spells in the open. You will have to consider all the different elements that surround you and take care of it while practicing Wiccan religion. It is clearly stated in the principles that it is important to stay away from harming others. Even if you dislike someone then it is not right to cast spells against them. Wicca should only be used to attain positive results.

Chapter 11: Precautions

Choose Carefully

It is understood that Wicca magic is quite powerful and can help with attaining all that you desire. But it will be important to make use of tools and equipment that are of top quality as they can provide the best results. Right from the tools such as the bells and candles to the offerings such as flowers and herbs, you must ensure to use all the best that is available to you. If you are picking these up yourself then it is best to inspect them first. If you are ordering online then look for a trustworthy site that have good reviews and testimonials. This will ensure you find yourself quality products.

Understand Power

It is essential to understand your own power before casting a spell. Do not summon anything that cannot be controlled. This can include powerful Gods and also certain spirits. If you are not sure how to appease them then it is best to avoid calling them. It will be a good idea to have someone help you out, especially if they are aware of how to control a certain situation. If at all you find yourself in such a situation then put in efforts to please the God and calm him down.

Partner

Many Wiccans prefer to team up with a partner in order to carry out the rituals effectively. But it will be important to understand the type of power that each one of you brings in. many times, two powerful entities will not be able to cast spells together as there will be a clash. It will be best for one of you to be a teacher and the other one be a student. This will make for a great combination and help the two of you cast good spells. It is also an option to join a Wiccan group. You will find like-minded people there who can help you avail a better experience with Wicca magic.

Expectations

It will be important to have reasonable expectations out of your practice. Some people end up having unreasonable expectations that will only lead to disappointment. Wicca magic works well no doubt but can take some time to show results and one must be patient with it. It only gets better with time and experience and so, patience will pay off positively.

Chapter 11: Precautions

Privacy

Remember that privacy is appreciated when it comes to magic. Dedicate a room for the practice or an area in the woods. Some people tend to make a show of it and perform it in a public place. This is not advisable as magic is a very personal practice. A quiet place in the woods or a corner spot on the beach are great to cast the spells.

Cleansing

Cleansing should be a part of your everyday routine. This is important to keep everything clean including the tools you use, the area used and yourself. Do not keep anything for tomorrow and do it as soon as you are done casting a spell. If you make use of any visual aid such as drawings and writings then wipe them off. Clean all the tools that were used and store them carefully for future use.

Chapter 12:
Cleansing Wiccan Tools and Instruments

In a previous chapter, we looked at the different tools that are used in Wicca. In this one, we will look at the ways in which you can cleanse the tools.

Herbs

One of the best and most preferred ways to cleanse tools is by using herbs. Herbs contain a form of natural energy that cleanse and chase away negativity. There are many types of herbs to choose from including rosemary, thyme and sage. Growing these in your garden will help you remain with a constant supply. Add a few fresh leaves to a bucket and place all the tools in it. Cover it with some more leaves and let it remain for 10 to 15 minutes. Once done, shake them gently and store safely.

Chapter 12: Cleansing Wiccan Tools and Instruments

Alternately, you may also burn the leaves and use the smoke to cleanse the tools. Add the leaves to a bowl or bucket and burn them for 2 minutes. Blow out the flame and move it around to spread evenly. Place the tools in it and allow it to stay overnight. But remember, the leaves should not be too hot lest they damage the tools. This method might not be ideal for fine silver as it might develop a black film.

Sea Salt

An easier option for those that do not have time to cleanse the tools using herbs is by making use of sea salt. Add the salt to a bucket and throw in the tools. Cover it completely with the salt and let it remain overnight. Some of the crystals in salt can be sharp so it will be best to remove such and then use the salt. Wearing gloves can help prevent scratches.

Crystals

Crystals can be quite effective in reducing negativity and cleaning the tools and equipment. There are many types of crystals to pick from with the most powerful one being black tourmaline. This can be added to a bowl along with other tools to cleanse them. The crystal absorbs all of the negative energy from it and cleanses it thoroughly. Once done, hold the crystal under running water to clean it.

Sun

One idea is to place the tools under the sun. The sun can be quite powerful and help in cleansing the tools thoroughly. Place them on a blanket and under the sun to cleanse thoroughly. But ensure that they will not get damaged under the sun. Keep them for 2 to 3 hours and store safely.

Moon

The moon is extremely powerful according to Wicca tradition and stands for the Goddess. One way of cleansing tools is by placing them under the moon for 3 nights. Add them to a bowl or place them over a blanket and let them soak in the moon rays. This will help in chasing away negativity and cleansing the tools. But remember to remove them in the mornings.

Mud Bath

Mud is a natural cleanser and can effectively diminish any negativity. It is also easily available and will make for a great cleansing option. Add fresh mud to a bucket and place the tools in it. Allow them to sit overnight. If you have a garden or backyard then bury the tools by digging a large enough hole in the ground. Place the tools and use a shovel to bury them. Mark the spot so that you know where to dig. Once done, use the shovel to remove the mud and take the tools out.

Blow

One easy way to cleanse tools and instruments is by simply blowing over them. Hold the instruments in your hand and gently blow over them. This should help in blowing away the negativity and cleansing them thoroughly. Pick an open space to perform the ritual preferably somewhere close to the sea. Refrain from doing it in a closed room as the negativity can loom within the walls. Face away from the wind and gently blow over the tools.

Water

Another quick fix is to run the tools under water. Hold them in your hand and place under running water. The water will help in cleansing away the negative energy from the tools. Some people also immerse it in hot water to reduce the negativity, but it is up to you to choose an option.

Remember that this should be treated as an indispensable part of your Wicca routine as it is important to cleanse the tools from time to time. Not doing so can cause hindrances in your practice. Make it a point to cleanse them as soon as a ritual is done so that they will be ready for use the next time.

It is important to take a little precaution while cleansing tools, as they can be sensitive and delicate.

It is interesting to note here that the same techniques can be used to cleanse your aura. If you think you have been affected by a negative entity then use any of the above methods to avail relief from it and brighten your aura.

Conclusion

I thank you once again for choosing this book and hope you had a fun time reading it.

The main purpose of this book was to educate you on the basics of Wicca magic and tell you how easy it is to adopt simple spells. Once you get started, you will start reaping its benefits and know exactly how powerful it is. Wicca is a form of white magic and should not be confused with black magic. It is extremely safe to take it up and will not affect you negatively. You need not stick with just these spells and can pick others based on your needs.

I hope you have all your dreams fulfilled by the application of Wicca magic.

Printed in Great Britain
by Amazon